I WANT TO BE A
GAME DEVELOPER

Written by
Jonathan Reule

Illustration
Phan Quỳnh Trang

Storyboard
Christiane Tee

First paperback edition October 2023
ISBN 978-981-17320-6-5

Published by Unibino Pte. Ltd.
9 North Buona Vista Drive, #02-01 Metropolis Tower 1, Singapore 138588

www.unibino.com

For many, gaming is a fun and exciting way to escape reality for a while. Whether enjoying fantastical realms, solving puzzles, or competing with friends, gaming can provide us all with a dose of good safe entertainment. That's why we value skilled game developers in our modern world.

Creating video games can be an enjoyable process, but it requires a great deal of effort, dedication, and imaginative thinking to bring them to life. So, if you're into gaming, programming, and creating new worlds and experiences, then perhaps being a game developer might be the right career for you!

But do you know why video games are so popular in our modern society? Well, much of it has to do with our inborn imaginations and our innate drive for competition. You see, since the beginning of time, we've used our imaginations to help explain the many natural phenomena occurring in our world.

Imagine if you suddenly saw a mountain explode, spewing red hot lava into the sky, without understanding scientifically what was going on. It's possible you might create a story around this occurrence. Perhaps it's a fiery monster living deep inside the volcano, growing angry at the people starting a village nearby its home? Or perhaps it's two gods fighting inside the mountain, causing plenty of damage in the process.

Regardless of the exact origins of these myths and tall tales, the fact remains that in the absence of scientific understanding, people often relied on their imaginations to fill in the blanks. This, of course, led to the creation of stories that were passed down from generation to generation - and became increasingly embellished over time.

Take the ancient Japanese belief in animism as an example. Animism is the idea that all things, including natural entities like mountains and rivers, possess spirits. This belief led to a rich tradition of folklore and mythology that incorporated these spirits into their stories, creating a world that is both familiar and yet fantastical at the same time. It's quite fun to imagine the forest being protected by a giant Tengu, flowing rivers full of mischievous Kappas, and foxes with nine-tails shapeshifting into humans!

While creativity and imagination play a significant role in the development of video games, our competitive attitudes have also been a driving force in their formation.

Human beings are wired to compete, and it has helped us survive by constantly pushing us to improve and reach our full potential. In fact, playing games of skill and chance has been commonplace for thousands of years to address this natural inclination we have for competition.

Ancient Egyptians were known for their love of games that people of all ages enjoyed. These games served not only as a source of entertainment but also helped in strengthening social bonds and promoting strategic thinking. Games like Hounds and Jackals, for instance, were similar to checkers and required players to think several moves ahead, while Senet was another popular board game that varied in its rules depending on which country it was played in.

Games were a common pastime during the Middle Ages, too, with several well-known games spreading across the world for everyone to enjoy. Among them was chess, which originated in India but found its way into countries all over the globe. The game was widely enjoyed, especially by the nobility, for how it challenged players to think critically and plan their moves carefully.

In addition to board games, outdoor sports and activities also became popular during the Middle Ages. Blind Man's Bluff was a game similar to tag, where one person would be blindfolded, trying to catch the other players who were calling to them. Archery was another popular outdoor activity, both for recreation and as a military training exercise. Even forms of folk football, similar to modern-day soccer, were played in the streets of medieval towns.

As you might be able to tell, many of these games carried on throughout the centuries and into modern times, which is a testament to our long-lasting desire to play fun and engaging games. Eventually, we created decks of cards, allowing us to make plenty of different types of games with only one deck of cards. But these card games often led to gambling and other forms of vice that some communities frowned upon.

This caused a demand for a different source of entertainment that wasn't associated with betting or other forms of presumed vice. In time, companies began taking notice of this gap in the market. One publishing company F. & R. Lockwood, made a note of this demand and went about designing and releasing the first US board game known as Travelers Tour through the United States. After this point, board games became commonplace in most American households and soon expanded into the rest of the world.

However, the real games were about to begin when in the late 1930s, the first working computers were invented. It wasn't long after this that scientists programmed a computer to play chess independently in 1951.

Although if we jump ahead to just a year later, 1952, we will find what many consider the very first video game ever created. This game was called OXO, developed by British professor of computer science Sandy Douglas. The video game was a basic interface of tic-tac-toe that could simulate X's and O's to play the classic game on a digital screen.

As groundbreaking as it was, unfortunately, OXO was never adopted by the masses, mainly due to the lack of personal technology at that time.

LEFT
RIGHT

This didn't stop people from experimenting and creating new video games, though. Take physicist William Higinbotham as an example - he created a virtual game in 1958 named Tennis for Two, where players could send a ball back and forth over a digital net with the chance of scoring enough points to win the match!

Soon, this trend of making independent video games started to take off, especially when some of these early games were showcased at technology exhibitions. Only four years after Tennis for Two was made and released, a group of MIT students came together and programmed a game for the PDP computer known as Spacewars!

It was the first time a video game became readily available to the masses - or at least anyone with a PDP computer. A lot of folks consider this to be a foundational game for the video game world, as it gave rise to more indie producers, who came out with new video games that would change the landscape of the entertainment world forever!

After this, developers started to realise that not everyone was going to own a PDP computer, yet they might still want to play these video games. So, these developers began making consoles that could house specific games to be played by anyone, whether they owned a computer or not. Pong was one of the first games to do this. With two simple knobs as controllers, players could play a virtual game of table tennis - for as long as they wanted. However, the creators at Atari weren't satisfied just yet. In 1975 they created a pong controller that could be hooked to a personal television and played at home.

Although this was another great breakthrough, it would be another decade before home consoles became a competitive item on the market. And as fun as pong was, it still had its limits as a video game. You could only hit the small ball back and forth for so long before seeking out other forms of entertainment to keep you busy. That's when the rise of arcade video games started their takeover.

What others may have seen as a passing fad, some savvy businessmen and women saw these virtual games as a money-making item. So that's when they set out to monetise on this new technology by founding companies that focused purely on creating these arcade video games. This was when competition flooded the video game market, and simple yet addictive games were highly sought after.

Companies such as Atari, Taito, Sega, and Midway Manufacturing, threw their hats into the arcade ring and began churning out some of the most iconic arcade machines of all time. From Pac-Man to Space Invaders to Donkey Kong and even Frogger, these arcade machines took the gaming world to a whole new level. People began spending bucket full of quarters just to try and achieve high scores, to show they were the best players around.

Before long, these video games moved from giant arcades to small portable consoles, where players could purchase individual titles that they could enjoy in the comfort of their own homes. Developing these games became a high priority for companies wanting to jump into the newest trend, which is when more programmers were hired, along with unique artists who could make pieces of art out of tiny square pixels. This wasn't all. Of course, video game companies wanted their titles to stand out when compared to their competitors, so they began hiring writers to make their games even more immersive for players.

This lucrative market led to more and more advances in video games. From 8-bit systems to 32-bit and even up to 64-bit graphics, all within the span of a decade. Soon video games were created over enormous virtual maps that could take players years to explore the entire layout. But developing these video games is not as easy as they may look. It takes a lot of hard work, effort, and skill to bring them to the finish line.

But this may have you wondering what it takes to be a game developer. Firstly, it's key to know what type of developer you'd like to be. There are programmers who help to make the game run smoothly, artists that create the different characters and the surrounding world, also are writers who help to add to the game's dialogue or come up with the entire plot for the narrative ahead of its creation.

No matter which route you choose, it's crucial that you take your role seriously and put in the best work you can so that you can grab the right opportunity when it may arise. Other than that, there are special degrees you can earn in game development or boot camps that can teach you how to design and program your own video game. There is also the option to try and apply at a big gaming company for a junior role to learn the ins and outs of the industry.

But what responsibilities do game developers have on a daily basis? That depends on your function in the entire process. If you are a part of the game's story and plot line, then you may be tasked to come up with a unique storyline to build the game upon. For example, you may create a game about a world where all the adults have suddenly turned into robots, and you must work together with other kids in order to solve the mystery and reclaim your parents!

If you are an artist, then you'll need to take those ideas and start designing the characters, the game's environment, and items found within the game. Or you may be one of the technical programmers that help to code the game's world, characters, powers, and any secrets hidden in plain sight!

It's also a good idea to try and decide what type of game you'd like to develop. There are several different genres, and each requires special layouts and features. There are RPG-type games, which often need lots of dialogue and written text to play, whereas open-world games may need more cutscenes or animations to keep the story progressing.

YOUR TEAM

Overall if you are planning to be the head developer for a game, you'll need to be good at overseeing each of these aspects that go with creating the video game. A good game developer will be able to communicate clearly and effectively with his or her team. That way, the product is completed at the right time and with the original vision intact.

Being a game developer requires a lot of hard work and dedication, just like any other job. You'll need to learn about programming, design, and game engines. But if you have a passion for creating games and are willing to put in the effort, then the future can be bright in this field.

Who knows, maybe one day you'll be a famous game developer, creating the next big hit game or hosting gaming competitions. Or you might wind up as a lead developer, managing a team of talented developers and designers. No matter what you choose, always give it your best and allow the rest to come in time.

My Inspiration

Shubhi Saxena
Founder, Unibino

As a parent in this ever-changing world, it can sometimes feel overwhelming when it comes to our children's futures. New technologies seem to be arising almost every day, and with so many innovations, it creates unique professions which many of us wouldn't have dreamed to be necessary only a few years ago. Which to me is a good thing. Because with so much variety, my children can have the opportunity to pick a career that will fit their personalities and build upon their strengths. As you may imagine, this desire within me to provide my children with the resources they needed to thrive, led me to search out books that would be easy enough for them to understand while teaching them about various professions.

Only, I found that these books were few and far between. Even if I could find a book about a certain profession geared towards young readers, I found them sparse inside and limited to only certain careers that may not fit my children's abilities. This is when I came up with the idea to write my own children's books, teaching them about all the various careers in the modern world. After months of researching different professions and learning more than I ever expected, I quickly realised this was going to be a bigger project than I first anticipated. I dove into the histories of these professions, discovering links to the past, and why these professions were now so important.

Ultimately my goal was to offer my children options, to show them that there is no one set path for everyone. But in this, I stumbled upon something bigger. I wanted to share this with future generations. To share with all children and parents about these careers, to help spark curiosity, and to instil a passion for the future. Everyone has special talents and abilities, and I hope that this series will be able to offer clarity and inspiration to children around the world. Because at the end of the day, it's never too early to start dreaming and never too late to take action. With this, I hope you enjoy this series and that your young ones become the best versions of themselves as they can achieve.